Replete

Vivacity

Replete Vivacity
by Eugene Lucas

Published by Moore & Poesy Publishing
Design by Yolanda Williams

Replete

Vivacity

Eugene
Lucas

Dear Readers,

I hope that this collection of poetry

fillings your soul with humor and tenderness

with an enjoyment to share.

Replete is to be filled and vivacity means

full of life . May each and everyone of you

be Replete Vivacity.

Eugene

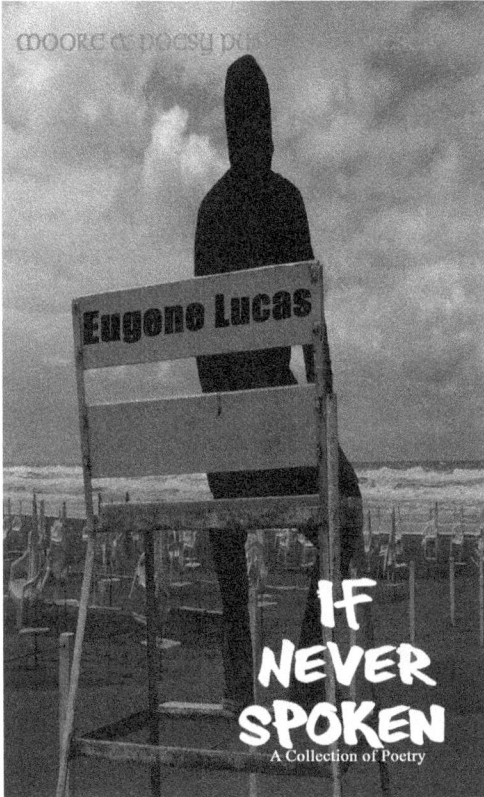

NOW AVAILBLE ON AMAZON KINDLE

Part 1

Behind Da Glass

Contents

Magic

I often thought of the paper
That traveled with the wind
How simple with its spin
Moving from one place to the another
I wish I had that cover
To clothed myself and disappear
Into the day or night
Landing wherever I like
To be simple as the paper
Flowing not knowing
Where it is going
I wish I had it
Magic
I wish

You & Air

Your body is as vivacious as the inside of
Your womb
Making a life bloom
Inside of you
To kiss your features
To feel your soul
Like floating feathers
Waiting to land
With my hands
A single breath
To be inside of you
Collecting the joyous
Tenderness as we sweat

A Whisper

Four walls
To keep my thoughts going
No sappy moment to not
Appreciate the hours
A sweet , sweet sound of
My heart beating
Within these walls
God don't leave me
My strength can only bend objects
Not faith or hope
My appearance can only be seen not
Tuck'd away in a bag full of old jeans
The relax sound as
My heart pounds with
The air in my lungs
Very thankful that I can hum

2 Meet There

As a man
My outlook is taken by
The social gathering of society
If I smile my ego is fragile as
A woman's pelvis bone
If I show no emotions
I am cold and unmoved to cry
With the world's madness
My prayers I send to God
Who has this world in his reach
A provider or a protector

My decision not to be
A hesitation to the land
To slide passion inside of a wet shell
With a curvy frame
Meeting there
In this untamed natural
With my mental activities
As a man who knows that
He isn't lost

Note

Precious soul, do you hear me ?
I speak to you
The ceiling above my head
The twin foam underneath my legs
There is no insane pause to
Try to fathom all of my words
Together as they come
Joy and laughter to send a note
To my soul
To keep me seeking after
Tranquility and gentle dreams

Date 2 Come Home

Don't want tears in your eyes
I want a big smile
When I arrive
Let no past memory of me
Have you sad my struggles
Have made me more humble as
A man to love you (my heart)

There is no pain when I meet you
With my mortal as
I have waited to reflect on
Your beauteous smile with
Rays in the clouds following you
Remember all of my words
That I have written to you
Heart to heart
We are in a rhythm flit
Moving quickly to
The sound of love (my love)
Be happy when we meet
My date to comfort
Your solitude terrene
Is near

Da Storm

Got a bullet in
My hand but I can't throw it
Got my hand on the trigger because
I can't control it
My mental part says, "R.I.P." to
The fake foot-walkers
D.I.E. no feet to run
When my words come
I see my son in a palm
Not a hand but on land
Smiling with no regrets
To rest in the sunset

My son, my li'l man
Your daddy will stand against
The monsoon for you
Let my words
Reach you always
No matter what the storm makes
My li'l man
You stand against
The opaque with prayer
To see me with love and my words
I love you
My li'l man
I love you (just stand)

Warm & Bright

Waltz with me (my darling)
Put your hand in mine
One foot at a time
Promise to make
Daisies present because
It's your favorite
You are amazing (my darling)
Capturing my every glance as
We move in our silence
If I tell you repeatedly that
I am in
A bottomless hole of love with you
I mean it
Truly I do
Take my hand and waltz with me
This evening (my darling)

Life 2 See

A collection of you in my mind
The different areas that
Your smile takes me to
In my recollection
I love you more
A slide down your curvaceous frame
With my hand
My recollection
I love you more
Flashes of you
Turning and laughing with life
Building a beautiful canvas in my mind
We connect with life as
I enjoy your smile

Behind Da glass

Sorrow to feel the tears that hide
With words that
Can't explain the evening
I know that you'll be leaving
So, I give my reasons
The clear slab reminds me
To be timely with my words
My heart wants to tell you more
My soul congealed
To your rivet eyes
I know this is not what you had in mind
A decent converse of the changes
My soul want let me do the explaining
My facial expression has the sentences

I want to say
This separation in my mind is hurtful
Because I can't touch you how I want to
The smell of your flesh
Wondering is that pussy wet
Frozen in with my thoughts as the
Time moves you to the door
So much more that I want to give you
To tell you that my heart lives with you
You're my succor
The man you see in front of you
Is dying inside with
An ambry of tears
Behind this glass
There is something to hope for
A doorway to be happy with you again

Part 2

2 Touch A Cloud

Contents

When U Think

Ponder with my dreams dark clouds
To make me scream
To my eyes opening
I miss you more than the letters
That I couldn't write to you
To repeat the same thing
When u think
My movement is ready to relax
In my cave with sports and a beverage
I hear you
You don't have to yell it

Pass Me By

As humble as I know how to be
A prayer to the greatest creator
With my rib bone
Your mercy made it clear
A clone made for me
To never be alone
Within a second it's gone
Like money lose on the streets
Snatched up by hands
A canteen and no privacy
A prayer to the greatest (the most high)
Please don't pass me by

How

To be sitting unattached from the world
The bench has the warmest embrace as
The tears roll underneath my skin
Where has it been?
How can it be seen?
The beautiful things that surrounds me
The undertone of the trees
The breeze that flows so freely
How can it be seen?
With your hand in mine
Can you trust me with your time?

The man that you seek
How can life be so calm and defeated all
in the same moment?
Sitting alone with my thoughts
Replete filled
Vivacity lively
To my outside frowning
My inner has a smile of peace
To the chapters closing
With a new story to read

Lock Down

The sound of the water drops
Hitting the porcelain
Making a song that my ears agree with
The scene of the hour
To fill up with my emotions
A picture of you close to my chest
Waiting for the light to
See your comely face
Staring back at me as the hours of sleep
Rolls with my thoughts
Across my heart your
Picture lights up my world with
Hope to see you again in the splendor

Da Outside

Simple as sand running through fingers
I wish it was
Easy as a leaf moving with no means
To complicated its destination
The joy of waiting to feel
The inside of you
Because you know
I've been a good boy
Like you wanted me to
I wish I knew
The truth about my future
Will you still be the present that I love
To unwrap or my past
Leaving me for another nigga?

Window

She knows me
But, will she notice me?
When her eyes see the agony in me
A reflection between us as we watch us
We both realize that we've missed us
All of the disagreements and
Not speaking until someone is leaving
We find ourselves envisage
Needing each others help
At the window

Sun in Da sky

Everyday to wake up inside of this place
To bring a smile to your face (my lady)
To shower me as
I taste you (my lady)
To deviate as you move your waist
Everyday, everyday
Making you feel this way
Everyday, everyday

Breath

Following your skin
That black lacy trail
Wrapped around your hips
My fingers found the courage
To not rip but pull
Your soft felt design aside
Like drinking from a succulent cactus
My tongue makes splashes
Apart with myself in the middle
A breath to take
Drinking from the inside of
Your waist

Strive

Ms. Lady ,if you feel unappreciated
If you feel like your
Skin, size or clothes are
Just apart of the wind blow
I appreciate you and
I love you
Although my words are in front of you
Your beautiful even if I can't see you
Without you life wouldn't have
It's full significant
The scent of your velvety skin tone
Day or night the bone in my pants
Can't leave you alone
Eating endive of french fries
I love your strive(Ms.Lady)
Your beauty
Is in my eyes

Part 3

If
(Poems 1-4)

Pt·1

If your looking for a rescue
The cape and the big letter S
Across the sternum
High price denim with
A mulish tenet like a
Nigga suppose to pay for it
If your looking for this
All you will get is dick
No sentiment

Pt· 2

If you want your heels to carry you
If you want your bills
To go far away from you
Can you manipulate the truth?
If you could see
The coming of time running
In your view
Would you obtain?

Pt· 3

If you knew
What the system would be like,
Would you believe in drying now?
The words that they say
The madness to drink up
If you knew
What would you chose,
If you knew the plan for you?

Pt. 4

If there is a bullet waiting for me
Let me be free
If there is a moist and thick
Piece of pussy waiting for me
Let me dive deep
If my soul can't find the comfort
To be with the sunrise
Give me time
If my thoughts can't handle the view
That plays with my manhood
Don't let me be lost
If there is a place to share my thoughts
Than let me be free

ABOUT THE AUTHOR

Eugene Lucas resides in Florida.
He is currently working on his second poetry
book, *The Winter I Remember*.

Eugene would love to hear from his fans
by mail.

Eugene Lucas -J37645
Calhoun Correctional Institution
19562 Institution Dr.
Blountstown, Fla 32424

MOORE & POESY PUBLISHING PRESENTS

KONCRETE

THOUGHTS

A COLLECTION OF POETRY

EUGENE LUCAS

FRIENDS + ENEMIES

I ain't that nigga
Made of steel
Just trying to hold on
To God's will

Kill or be killed
Shit! The struggle is real
I know how to deal with how
I feel about the
Light and the darkness

I ain't that nigga
Trying to be the hardest
My garden ain't full of fresh
Fruits and shit
If you blink wrong I'll shot

So how can I trust you?
In my mind set
The devil is on every set
But I say,"Lord order my steps."

My concept to reject
My guess to never test
An enemy over family
Friends over situations
Because a character

Will take ya to that decision road
Some shit and some people
You gotta let go

I ain't that nigga
Speaking and seeking
Shit with no benefits
The ground level is a quest
To rise above to see
The field of riches
People wanna feel quickly
You know get something out of a deal

But I pray, "Lord order my steps."
Keep me in your will
It's funny how money
Can bring change
Loose coins to join a wide road
To be known and the ground level
Always has been looked away

To find nothing but yourself
Being alone it's funny
How friends + enemies play
The same games
But I say, "Lord don't take your joy
away."

GOLDTEETH

Flashin' when I was dashin'
A nigga got all of the
Women eye lashes
My dreads turnt heads and my tint
Made heads swirl as I bent corners

Damn, a nigga had bands
But now without the cow
Alone and I hear my
Own voice singing a song

With four walls
Nobody called
No one is listening to my melody
Behind this concrete

Heavenly because I had to
See the shit ain't sweet
The streets didn't love me
They loved my gold teeth

To find me in the streets
I was no different from
The next nigga sittin'
In some chrome feet

But my situations
Made questions to the answers
That I was seeking

Nobody called me
No one heard me speak
Until that DC number
Recognized me with daily
Messages that I can't delete

I had to see
The streets didn't love me
They loved my gold teeth

ME THE VIEW

Truth I called you
Reality I saw you too
Morals I had a few + I understand u

What you do to my view?
You never lied about proof
People will change on you

Love I feel you deeply
Lies you put the fear in my eyes
But hope you made me be aware
That someone does care

About faith? I can't wait
But like all things I gotta maintain
Being there to share my pain
A purpose to choose
Me the view

GOOD THOUGH

This ain't no prison talk
But I love the way you walk
In my mind I often
Think about that spine

Covered with cinnamon
Smelling all fruity and shit
Sweet remembrance
When we made heat

I fuck'd you on the stove
Head, knees and toes
Spread out with my dick and fingers In
that mouth you never tapped out

Moved you to the fridge
To cool ya off
You was good at taking this dick
No rules and I put it all around you

Though you never said it
I knew that this dick was
Good to you

The way I put dem nutts to you
Hands to hips
Firm with my grip
Sixty-nine all lips

Remember you love'd
The way I use to sip that
Pussy juice sticking
My thumb in it
Sample sprinkle I was an animal
That pussy was my harvest
Collecting juice good though

TRUTH BRONCO

No fish bowl
I had black screens
Man my bronco was clean

Girls couldn't wait to be seen
I had no problems
Getting into their jeans
Man my bronco was clean

I had my tires saturated
With oil glossy blind
When my feet hit the gas
Dem hoes pussy had
A tingle sensation
When I hopped out
With gold faces

Got a standing ovation
When I drove pass
The people waiting
Man that was a good situation

When the sun was out
I was never bakin'
Dew so cold
Made dem hoes nipple hard like coal
No dirty bricks in my shit
I had that Taco Bell money
I was never hungry
Cheesy and life made
A laughable moment
To bring shame and rain
I had a aim
I was working in the game
The streets knew my name
But got damn
My bronco held the stage

DOUBLE NACHO

I took a look around
To see the sauce gone
Now, I know where I belong

When I was cheesy
The streets they feared me
Broke niggas couldn't get near me

The ground was
Collecting empty shells and I
Was at Taco Bell
Doing well

A jealous ass nigga
Cast'd a spell and all
I see now is a canteen and my cell

Trade for that good grade
"A", of course with these four walls
This twin mattress
I'm waiting on the right reaction

Cover them shells
With some beef
Because nigga's today
Are scared to flex with their feet

Quick to pull some heat but
Here I am waiting on relief
Am I innocent or guilty?
I'll let God judge me

I ain't throwing salt
I killed that nigga
Before he got caught

*****

In, Koncrete Thoughts...within the reach of...one
solid hour. One recollection with verses. One solid
reasoning. Many entities of its events.The ups and
downs of its universe.

Koncrete Thoughts
By Eugene Lucas

www.ingramcontent.com/pod-product-compliance
Lightning Source LLC
Chambersburg PA
CBHW020527030426
42337CB00011B/573